EMAIL MARKETING SECRETS

Discover Proven Techniques to Boost Sales and Engage Customers!

Ray Goodwin

CONTENTS

LIABILITY DISCLAIMER

The information contained within this book is intended for informational purposes only and should not be construed as legal or professional advice. The authors and publishers of this book are not responsible for any losses or damages that may arise from the use of the information contained within.

The reader assumes full responsibility for any decisions made based on the information in this book. The authors and publishers do not endorse any particular method, service or product mentioned in this book and are not responsible for any consequences resulting from their use.

The reader should exercise caution and discretion when making life changing decisions, and should be aware of the risks and potential consequences of their actions. This book is not a substitute for professional or legal advice and should not be relied upon as such.

By reading and using the information in this book, the reader acknowledges and agrees to hold harmless the authors, publishers, and any other parties involved in the creation or distribution of this book from any and all liability, claims, damages, or losses that may arise from their use of the information contained herein.

CHAPTER 1: INTRODUCTION TO EMAIL MARKETING

Welcome to Email Marketing Secrets, where you'll discover the tried and true methods for turning your email list into a lucrative sales tool. As someone with 25 years of experience in online sales, I have seen first-hand how powerful email marketing can be when executed correctly.

In this book, I will share my secrets on how to build a strong email list that actually converts into sales. You'll learn about crafting compelling subject lines and email copy that entices your subscribers to open your messages.

But it's not just about getting people to open your emails - it's also about providing value and building trust with your audience. That's why I'll delve into the importance of segmenting your list and sending targeted messages that speak directly to each subscriber's interests.

And don't forget about the technical side of things! From choosing an email service provider to understanding deliverability rates, I'll guide you through all the necessary steps to ensure your emails reach their intended inbox.

So sit back, grab a notebook, and get ready to master the art of email marketing!

Overview

Marketing is about reaching out to the right people, at the right time, with the right message. And there is no denying that email marketing is one of the most effective ways to do that. It allows you to establish a direct line of communication with your target audience, and engage with them on a more personal level.

So, what exactly is email marketing? And how can it help your business?

Definition of Email Marketing

Email marketing is the process of using email to promote your products or services, and build relationships with your target audience. It involves sending commercial messages to a group of people who have explicitly or implicitly given their permission to receive such communication.

Email marketing can take many forms, including newsletters, promotional offers, event invitations, and surveys. It can be used for a variety of purposes, such as lead generation, customer retention, sales promotion, and brand awareness.

Importance of Email Marketing in Business

Email marketing is one of the most cost-effective and measurable forms of marketing. It allows you to reach out to a large audience at a fraction of the cost of traditional advertising methods. And with the help of analytics, you can track the effectiveness of your campaigns, and make data-driven decisions to optimize your strategy.

Statistics and Benefits of Email Marketing

Let's take a look at some statistics and benefits of email marketing:

❖ According to a study by DMA, email marketing generates an average ROI of $38 for every $1 spent.

❖ Email marketing is 40 times more effective at acquiring new customers than Facebook or Twitter, according to McKinsey.

❖ 81% of B2B marketers use email newsletters for content marketing, according to Content Marketing Institute.

❖ 59% of marketers say that email is their biggest source of ROI, according to HubSpot.

❖ Personalized emails have a 29% higher open rate and 41% higher click-through rate than non-personalized ones, according to Campaign Monitor.

Different Types of Email Marketing

Email marketing can be divided into different types, depending on the purpose and content of the email. Let's take a look at some of the most common ones:

❖ Promotional Emails: These are emails that promote your products or services, and offer discounts or special deals.

❖ Newsletter Emails: These are regular emails that provide updates, news, and tips related to your industry or niche.

❖ Event Invitation Emails: These are emails that invite subscribers to events, such as webinars, seminars, or product launches.

❖ Survey Emails: These are emails that seek feedback from subscribers, and help you understand their preferences and needs.

❖ Welcome Emails: These are emails that welcome new subscribers to your list, and introduce them to your brand and offerings.

Overview of the Book

In this book, we will dive deep into the world of email marketing, and explore the different strategies and techniques that can help you leverage this powerful medium to grow your business. From building an email list to creating compelling content, from setting up automation workflows to tracking and analyzing your campaigns, we will cover everything you need to know to succeed in email marketing.

Setting up Email Marketing Goals

Before you start with your email marketing campaign, it's important to set up goals for your campaign. These goals will help you to measure the effectiveness of your campaign and make necessary changes if required.

Your goals can be anything from increasing your subscriber base to generating more sales for your business. Once you have set up the goals, you need to ensure that all the elements of your email campaign are aligned with the goals.

Setting up Email Marketing Budget

Email marketing is one of the most cost-effective marketing channels, but it does require some investment. Depending on the size of your business and the scale of your campaign, you need to allocate a budget for various elements of your email marketing campaign.

These elements may include email automation software, email templates, lead magnets, email copywriting, email design, and email analytics. By setting up a budget, you can ensure that you have enough resources to run a successful email marketing campaign.

Choosing an Email Marketing Platform

The success of your email marketing campaign depends largely on the email marketing platform you choose. There are many email marketing platforms available in the market, each with its own set of features and pricing.

When choosing an email marketing platform, you need to consider factors such as ease of use, scalability, integration with other tools, analytics, and customer support. Some of the popular email marketing platforms include Mailchimp, Constant Contact, Campaign Monitor, and Aweber.

In conclusion, email marketing is a powerful tool that can help you achieve your business goals and connect with your audience on a deeper level. And with the right strategies and techniques, you can leverage this medium to achieve great results. The rest of the book will cover everything you need to know to succeed in email marketing.

CHAPTER 2: BUILDING AN EMAIL LIST

Email marketing has proven to be one of the most effective ways to reach customers and generate sales. However, it all starts with building a responsive email list. In this chapter, we will explore the best practices for creating an email list that can convert leads into sales. We'll go through defining your target audience, understanding where and how to collect email addresses, creating lead magnets, generating social media leads, creating landing pages, segmenting your email list, maintaining a clean email list, and growing your list.

Defining your target audience

Defining your target audience is the first step in creating an email list. You can't send emails if you don't know the people you want to send them to. Defining your target audience will enable you to conduct smart email marketing campaigns that will result in more leads and higher conversion rates. Questions you need to ask yourself when defining your target audience include:

- ❖ What is the demographic of my ideal customer?

- ❖ What are my potential customer wants and pain points?

- ❖ What topics will my ideal customer be interested in?

With these questions in mind, you'll have a clearer picture of the audience you're trying to reach with your email marketing campaigns.

Best practices for collecting email addresses

Building an email list that converts is not a one-time event. Therefore, you need to invest the effort to collect email addresses at every point of contact with potential customers. Here are some of the most effective ways to collect email addresses:

- ➢ Use pop-ups and forms on your website - One of the most effective ways to collect email addresses is by using pop-ups and forms on your website. You can use tools like OptinMonster and Sumo to create visually appealing pop-ups and forms that convert.

- ➢ Use social media to collect emails - Social media is a powerful tool to engage with your audience. You can use Facebook, Instagram, Twitter, and LinkedIn ads to target your ideal customers with messaging and lead magnets, helping to grow your list.

- ➢ Host events and webinars - Hosting an event or webinar is a great way to engage with potential customers and share your products and services. Collecting email addresses at the event or webinar with a lead magnet can work well.

- ➢ Run contests and giveaways - Running a contest or giveaway and asking for participants to provide their email address to participate can be a powerful way to add new subscribers.

Creating lead magnets

Lead magnets are a way to entice users to provide their email addresses. They can be freebies such as e-books, case studies, or white papers that provide value to subscribers. You can also offer exclusive access to special deals or promotions. The key is to offer something that entices potential customers to provide their email. Ideally, your lead magnet should provide value and speak to your target audience. To create effective lead magnets:

❖ Identify pain points - Your lead magnet should solve a specific problem faced by your target audience.

❖ Offer targeted solutions - Provide actionable steps to solve the problems your target audience faces.

❖ Keep it simple - Keep the messaging and design of your lead magnet simple and clear.

Utilizing social media for list building

Social media platforms like Facebook, Instagram, and LinkedIn can be an excellent source of subscribers. You can use paid ads, promoted posts, and organic engagement campaigns to reach your target audience. However, it's important to know the best practices for utilizing social media for list building:

❖ Post consistently - Regularly sharing valuable content on social media will help you gain followers and increase engagement.

❖ Interact with your audience - Engage with existing followers and potential customers to build trust and establish relationships.

Landing pages and opt-in forms

Landing pages and opt-in forms are effective tools for capturing email addresses. A landing page is a dedicated page on your website where you offer your lead magnet. An opt-in form is a section on your website where visitors can provide their email address to access the lead magnet. To create effective landing pages and opt-in forms:

❖ Simplify the design - Opt-in forms and landing pages should be aesthetically pleasing, simple and easy to navigate.

❖ Emphasize the lead magnet - The lead magnet should be the main focus of your landing page and opt-in form messaging.

❖ Include a strong CTA - Include a call-to-action that encourages your audience to provide their email address.

Segmenting your email list

Segmenting your email list is essential for effective email marketing. It involves dividing your email list into smaller groups based on specific characteristics such as interests, location, and engagement with your emails. Doing so will enable you to send targeted messages to each group rather than generic emails that may not engage the individual subscribers effectively.

Maintaining a clean email list

A clean email list is critical for effective email marketing. You should regularly monitor the email addresses on your list to ensure that you aren't sending emails to invalid addresses or inactive subscribers. The following tools can assist with maintaining a clean email list:

- Email verification - Email verification services can identify invalid email addresses, preventing you from sending emails to inactive or fake addresses.

- Email validation - Services that validate your email content can detect and fix issues such as spam triggers, avoiding email providers' spam filters.

- Email hygiene - Utilize email hygiene tools to remove bounces, spam traps, and duplicate email addresses from your email list.

Growing your email list

Your email list will naturally shrink over time. Customers unsubscribe, email addresses become invalid, and other reasons can contribute to the list dwindling. Therefore, it's essential to regularly grow your email list. Here are some tips to achieve growth:

- ❖   Offer more lead magnets - Provide multiple lead magnets for each customer persona to provide additional opportunities to grow your email list.

- ❖   Run social media campaigns - Use organic or paid social media campaigns to promote your offer and grow subscriber numbers.

- ❖   Offer exclusive content – Provide exclusive newsletters, promotions, and discounts to subscribers to provoke urgency to join.

Conclusion

A well-targeted and effectively maintained email list is integral to your email marketing success. By applying the best practices in collecting email addresses, segmenting your list, and maintaining a clean list, you can engender trust and foster engagement over time. Always remember to offer value to your customers and personalize your messaging to improve your chances of conversion.

CHAPTER 3: EMAIL CONTENT

In the digital age, where inboxes are flooded with countless emails daily, it is crucial to ensure that your email content is compelling and captivating to the reader. Email content is a crucial element of the email marketing campaign. Effective email content can make the difference between your emails being opened, clicked through, and acted upon or just being deleted. Therefore, it is essential to know the different types of email content, how to write effective subject lines, the importance of personalization, crafting call-to-actions, avoiding spam filters, and best practices for formatting and design.

Types of Email Content

When it comes to email marketing, it's important to mix up the various types of content to keep your audience engaged. Here are a few popular types of email marketing content:

1. Promotional Emails

Promotional emails are the most common type of email marketing content. These emails are designed to promote a product or service and drive sales conversion. They often contain discount codes, special offers, and other limited-time deals.

2. Newsletter Emails

Newsletter emails aim to provide subscribers with valuable information on a regular basis, such as industry updates, company news, and exclusive updates about the business. These emails are often sent weekly or monthly, depending on the business.

3. Welcome Emails

Welcome emails are sent to new subscribers, thanking them for signing up and welcoming them to your community. These emails can contain a discount code for a first purchase, a rundown of your most popular products, or a quick guide to your services.

4. Event Invitation Emails

Event invitation emails are sent to subscribers to invite them to upcoming events, such as webinars, networking events, or product launches. These emails can contain a call-to-action (CTA) button to register for the event or sign up for a newsletter.

5. Review Request Emails

Review request emails are sent to customers who have recently made a purchase, requesting them to leave a review on the business website. These emails can contain links to the review platform or include a short survey to gather feedback.

Writing Effective Subject Lines

The subject line is the first impression of your email. It is what an individual reads before opening the email, so it is essential to make them catchy and impactful. Here are four tips for writing effective subject lines:

1. Keep it Short

The subject line should be concise and to the point. A common rule for a subject line is to keep it under 50 characters.

2. Personalize it

Personalized subject lines can increase open rates. Make use of your customers' names or previous purchase history to craft personalized subject lines to catch their attention.

3. Use Urgency

Creating a sense of urgency can make subscribers act fast. Highlight the limited availability of a product, or limited-time offers can be a great way to encourage conversions.

4. Be Creative

Think outside the box when crafting your subject lines. Using humor, puns, or rhyme to make your emails stand out in a crowded inbox.

The Importance of Personalization

Personalization is one of the most effective ways to increase engagement and drive sales in email marketing. Personalization aims to add a personal touch to each email, making it more relevant to the recipient. Here are some ways you can personalize your email content:

1. Make It Personal

Addressing the contact by name or including details that you know about them, such as their location, can make your emails feel more personal.

2. Use Segmentation

Segmentation is the process of dividing your email list into groups, so your emails are more relevant to your audience's interests. This can be based on demographics or their behavior on your website.

3. Customize Content

By combining personalized data with dynamic content, you can tailor each email to the recipient's specific interests. You can use personalized product recommendations or targeted content related to their recent purchases.

Crafting Compelling Email Copy

Your email copy should be engaging and persuasive, while also being concise and straightforward. Follow these tips to achieve effective email copy:

1. Show Meaningful Benefits

Make sure that your email contains informative and clear benefits to the recipient. This could be discounts, free shipping, or product benefits.

2. Keep a Conversational Tone

Use language that feels like a conversation, write like you are addressing someone in person, not just pushing a sale.

3. Use Storytelling

People remember stories more than facts. Tell a story in your email copy to make it more memorable.

4. Focus on the Call-to-action

A call-to-action (CTA) is the action you want your reader to take, such as clicking a button or purchasing a product. Make sure that your CTA button stands out and is easy to use.

Developing a Brand Voice

A brand voice is the tone and personality of your brand that runs through all your communication, advertising, and marketing. A strong brand voice can make the audience feel connected to your brand on a deeper level. Here are some tips to help you develop your brand voice:

1. Know Your Audience

Understand your ideal customer, their values, preferences, and what resonates with them so that your brand voice is in tune with them.

2. Be Consistent

Consistency is essential when developing a brand voice. Make sure that all of your communication, including emails, is written in the same tone and voice.

3. Create Guidelines

Create brand voice guidelines to ensure that everyone in your organization writes with the same tone. These guidelines should include the language, style, and tone you use in your emails.

Crafting a Call-to-Action

A call-to-action (CTA) is a phrase designed to prompt an immediate response or encourage a sale. A CTA should be clear, concise, and easy to find. Here are some tips for creating a CTA:

1. Use a Strong Action Word

A strong action word can increase the chances of your customer taking the desired action, such as "Buy Now" or "Get Yours."

2. Make it Visually Noticeable

Use contrasting colors or make the CTA button larger to stand out and make it easy for customers to find.

3. Avoid Generic CTA Phrases

Avoid generic and bland CTA phrases, such as "Learn More" or "Click Here." Make your CTA stand out, and tell customers exactly what will happen when they click it.

Avoiding Spam Filters

Spam filters, or junk email filters, are designed to protect email users from unwanted or unsolicited emails. To avoid being marked as spam, follow these tips:

1. Keep Your Email List Current

Remove any inactive subscribers or addresses that always bounce to ensure that you are not sending unwanted emails.

2. Avoid Spam Trigger Words

Avoid using words that trigger spam filters, such as "Free" or "Discount." Also, avoid using all capital letters in the subject line.

3. Provide an Easy Opt-Out Option

Make sure that you have an unsubscribe link in all your emails, and ensure that your readers can opt-out with a single click.

Best Practices for Formatting and Design

The visual presentation of your email content can make a significant difference in engagement rates. Here are some best practices to follow:

1. Use a Clean and Simple Design

A clean and simple design will increase readability and make it more visually appealing.

2. Optimize for Mobile Viewing

Ensure that your emails are mobile-friendly and easy to view on smartphones or tablets.

3. Use HTML and Text Versions

Include both HTML and text versions of your email content in case the HTML version is not supported by the recipient's email provider.

Conclusion:

Well-crafted email content is the backbone of an email marketing campaign. By understanding the different types of email content, writing effective subject lines, personalization, crafting compelling emails, and utilizing a strong brand voice and call-to-actions, you can create engaging emails that produce results. Ensure that you avoid spam filters, follow best practices for formatting and design, test your emails, and analyze performance to achieve optimal results.

CHAPTER 4: EMAIL CAMPAIGN STRATEGY

Email marketing campaigns are a crucial aspect of any business's marketing strategy. These campaigns are designed to engage with subscribers, generate leads, promote brand awareness, and ultimately drive conversions. In this chapter, we will explore the various email campaign strategies that businesses can utilize to achieve their marketing goals.

Setting up Email Automation

Email automation is the process of sending targeted emails to subscribers based on their behavior or actions. Automation can be triggered by a variety of actions, such as subscribing to a newsletter, making a purchase on the website, or abandoning a shopping cart. Automated emails are crucial for improving the overall customer experience by providing relevant and personalized information to subscribers, leading to increased customer engagement and satisfaction.

Understanding the Sales Funnel

The sales funnel is a methodical approach to guiding a prospect through the buying journey. The funnel consists of several stages, including awareness, interest, consideration, intent, and finally conversion. Email campaigns must align with the sales funnel, providing subscribers with the right information at the right time to nudge them towards conversion. Understanding the sales funnel is crucial for creating effective email campaigns that target customers at each stage of the funnel.

Creating Welcome Series

A welcome series is a series of automated emails that are sent to new subscribers, designed to introduce them to the brand and nurture them towards the first purchase. Welcome emails have an open rate of up to 91%, making them one of the most opened types of emails. A welcome series should include a friendly welcome message, an introduction to the brand, and a clear call to action.

Nurturing Your Leads with Drip Campaigns

Drip campaigns are automated emails that are sent to subscribers over an extended period at regular intervals. Drip campaigns are an excellent way to keep subscribers engaged while reducing the workload of manual email marketing. Drip campaigns are very effective, with open rates that are over 80% higher than single-send campaigns.

Running Promotional Campaigns

Promotional campaigns are designed to promote a specific product or service and generate leads or sales. Promotional campaigns can be launched for a variety of reasons, such as celebrating a milestone, seasonality, or even to boost sales during a slow period. Promotional campaigns must have a clear goal, a captivating subject line, and an attractive offer.

Utilizing Segmentation for Targeted Campaigns

Segmentation is the process of dividing your email list into different groups based on their interests, behavior, or preferences. Segmentation is essential for creating targeted campaigns that provide subscribers with relevant information, leading to increased engagement and conversions. Segmentation can be done based on several factors, such as demographics, location, purchase history, and behavior.

Creating Win-Back Campaigns

A win-back campaign is designed to re-engage subscribers who have gone inactive. Win-back campaigns are an excellent opportunity to revive a stale email list and boost engagement rates. Win-back campaigns should be personalized, acknowledging the subscriber's previous interactions with the brand and encouraging them to take action.

Setting up Abandoned Cart Emails

Abandoned cart emails are designed to remind customers about old shopping carts and encourage them to complete their purchase. Abandoned cart emails have an open rate of approximately 46% and a click-through rate of 13.8%, making them a highly effective campaign. Abandoned cart emails should have an engaging subject line, a clear call to action, and an incentive to complete the purchase.

Conclusion

Email campaign strategy is essential to the success of any email marketing campaign. With the right campaign strategy, businesses can achieve their marketing goals while engaging with subscribers effectively. Automated emails, drip campaigns, and promotional campaigns are just a few of the email campaign strategies that businesses can utilize to achieve their marketing objectives. Understanding the sales funnel, segmentation, and analytics is crucial for creating effective email campaigns that drive conversions and improve customer engagement.

CHAPTER 5: EMAIL ANALYTICS AND TESTING

Email marketing can be a highly effective strategy for growing your business, but it's important to track your metrics and ensure you are making data-driven decisions. Without proper tracking, it's impossible to know whether your emails are performing well or not, and you may miss opportunities to optimize your campaigns for better results.

This chapter will cover email analytics and testing, including how to measure campaign effectiveness, how to conduct A/B testing, and how to troubleshoot issues. With these techniques, you can improve the performance of your email campaigns and see better results.

Understanding Email Analytics

Email analytics provide valuable information about how your email campaigns are performing. By tracking the right metrics, you can gain insights into how your subscribers are interacting with your emails and use this information to improve your campaigns. Here are some key metrics to track:

Open Rates: The open rate measures the percentage of people who opened your email. This is a critical metric because it shows whether your subject line and sender name are compelling enough to prompt people to open your messages.

Click-Through Rates: The click-through rate measures the percentage of people who clicked on a link within your email. This is a crucial metric, as it shows how engaged your subscribers are with your content. If your click-through rate is low, it may be an indicator that your email content needs improvement.

Conversion Rates: The conversion rate measures the percentage of people who took the desired action, such as making a purchase or filling out a form, after clicking through to your website. This is the ultimate goal of your email campaign, so it's important to track your conversion rate to determine its effectiveness.

Unsubscribe Rates: The unsubscribe rate measures the percentage of people who have unsubscribed from your email list after receiving an email. If your unsubscribe rate is high, it may be a sign that your email content is not resonating with your audience.

Revenue: Revenue is an important metric to track since it shows the return on investment (ROI) of your email campaigns. By tracking revenue, you can determine whether your email campaigns are generating a positive return on your investment.

Analyzing Email Metrics

After collecting data on your email campaigns, it's crucial to analyze it to determine what is working and what is not. By finding patterns in your data, you can determine what elements of your campaigns are driving engagement and revenue. Here are a few tips to get the most out of your email analytics:

Compare metrics across campaigns: By comparing metrics across campaigns, you can determine what elements are working well across your audience. This may include subject lines, calls-to-action, or design elements.

Look for patterns in your data: Identifying patterns in your data may help you identify trends that can inform your email marketing strategy. For example, if you notice a spike in revenue after sending a particular type of email, you may want to consider doing more of that going forward.

Track metrics over time: By tracking metrics over time, you can determine how your email campaigns are performing over the long-term. This may help you make informed decisions about changes to your email campaigns.

A/B Testing

A/B testing, also known as split testing, involves testing two different versions of your email campaign to determine which one performs better. By A/B testing, you can determine the optimal elements of your email campaigns. Here are some elements to consider when conducting A/B testing:

Subject lines: Testing different subject lines can help you determine which ones encourage more open rates.

Email content: Testing different content, such as the length of the email or the placement of images and links, can help you determine the most engaging formats for your audience.

Calls-to-action: Testing different calls-to-action, such as button placement or color, can help you determine which ones encourage the most clicks.

Segmentation: Testing different email campaigns for segmented audiences can help you determine which messaging resonates with specific subsets of your audience.

When conducting A/B testing, it's important to test only one element at a time to accurately determine which element is driving engagement. By making incremental changes, you can continue to improve your email campaigns over time.

Improving Email Deliverability

Email deliverability is a crucial aspect of email marketing. You may have a great email campaign, but if it doesn't reach your subscribers' inbox, it won't be effective. Here are some tips for improving your email deliverability:

Authenticate your email: Email authentication is the process of verifying that your email is actually from you. By authenticating your email using SPF and DKIM, you can increase the likelihood that your email will be delivered to your subscribers' inbox.

Maintain a clean email list: Regularly removing unengaged subscribers and inactive email addresses can help improve your deliverability. This is because ISPs will often route emails to the spam folder if they receive a large number of bounces or complaints.

Avoid spam triggers: Avoid using spam trigger words and phrases in your email content, such as "free," "limited time," or "act now." These may trigger spam filters and prevent your email from reaching your subscribers' inbox.

Test your email before sending: Testing your email before sending can help identify issues that may prevent it from being delivered. This includes checking for broken links and ensuring that your email content is properly formatted.

Troubleshooting Issues

Email marketing isn't always foolproof, so it's important to have a plan in place for troubleshooting any issues that arise. Here are some common issues you may encounter:

Low open rates: Low open rates may be an indicator that your subject line or sender name needs improvement. Consider testing different subject lines or sender names to see if this improves your open rates.

Low click-through rates: Low click-through rates may be an indicator that your email content needs improvement. Consider testing different email content or calls-to-action to determine what drives the most engagement.

Low conversion rates: Low conversion rates may be an indicator that your email content isn't driving subscribers to take the desired action. Consider testing different messaging and calls-to-action to see what is most effective.

High unsubscribe rates: High unsubscribe rates may be an indicator that your email content isn't resonating with your audience. Consider surveying your subscribers to determine what types of content they would like to receive.

Conclusion

Email analytics and testing are important aspects of any email marketing campaign. By tracking your metrics and making data-driven decisions, you can improve your campaigns and see better results. With A/B testing, tracking metrics over time, and troubleshooting common issues, you can create effective email campaigns that engage your audience, increase your revenue, and grow your business.

CHAPTER 6: LIST MANAGEMENT AND COMPLIANCE

Email marketing regulations are constantly changing, and it's important for businesses to stay up-to-date on compliance to avoid potential legal issues and damaging their company's reputation. This chapter covers the various compliance issues businesses must adhere to, such as anti-spam laws, GDPR, and handling unsubscribe requests. It also discusses best practices for list management, including managing bounces and complaints and avoiding email blacklists.

Understanding Email Regulations

The first step in email marketing compliance is understanding the regulations that govern email marketing. The most important regulation that all businesses need to abide by is the CAN-SPAM Act, a set of rules established by the Federal Trade Commission (FTC) that applies to all commercial emails sent in the US. The CAN-SPAM Act lays down certain guidelines for email marketers, including:

❖ Including an unsubscribe link or a clear and conspicuous opt-out mechanism in all commercial emails.

❖ Disclosing your business name and the physical postal address of your business.

❖ Avoiding misleading subject lines or misleading content that is not relevant to the subject line.

❖ Including a clear identification that the email is an advertisement.

❖ Ensuring that the email is sent from a legitimate email address.

❖ Honoring opt-out requests within 10 business days.

❖ Being responsible for the actions of third-party partners when they send emails on your behalf.

It's also important for businesses to be aware of GDPR (General Data Protection Regulation), which applies to all businesses that collect data from EU citizens. GDPR provides guidelines and standards for data privacy, and email marketers must ensure that their practices are GDPR compliant, or they risk being fined heavily.

Complying with Anti-Spam Laws

Anti-spam laws prohibit email marketers from sending unsolicited emails. The CAN-SPAM Act requires that businesses only send marketing emails to recipients who have given their express or implied consent to receive email communications. This means that businesses must have a permission-based list of email subscribers. The consent should ideally come with a double opt-in process, where users first subscribe to a list and then confirm their subscription via email.

Another important aspect of compliance with anti-spam laws is that businesses must ensure that their emails are not marked as spam. Some email clients like Gmail and Outlook have built-in spam filters, and if your email is marked as spam too often, it can cause problems with email deliverability. To avoid this, businesses must ensure that their emails are accurately targeting their subscriber base, deliver valuable content, and are sent with a consistent frequency.

Handling Unsubscribe Requests

Every email sent by a business should include an unsubscribe link. The unsubscribe link should be noticeable and easily accessible for subscribers. The CAN-SPAM Act requires businesses to honor opt-out requests within 10 business days, but it's best to process them immediately.

Unsubscribes are natural and should not be taken too personally. Business owners should view this as a chance to keep their list clean and concentrate on maintaining quality subscribers while reducing email counts and lowering the risk of spam reports.

Managing Bounces and Complaints

Email marketers need to monitor their email bounce rates, which are the number of emails that are returned as undeliverable. There are two types of bounces: hard and soft. Hard bounces occur when emails are sent to an invalid email address, while soft bounces occur when an email address temporarily can't be reached (like a full inbox). It's important to remove hard bounces from your email list since they can adversely affect your email deliverability.

Another important aspect of list management is managing spam complaints. If a significant number of subscribers mark an email as spam, it can trigger spam filters and cause email deliverability issues. To minimize complaints, ensure that your content is relevant and offers value to your subscribers.

Protecting Your Email List

A clean email list is crucial for the effectiveness of email marketing campaigns. This means that businesses must ensure that their list is free from invalid addresses, fake accounts, and other spammy elements. In addition, businesses should never purchase email lists since it breaches anti-spam laws and can impact the brand's credibility.

The best way to protect your email list is to use double opt-in processes, maintain a regular email sending schedule, and provide quality and relevant information. By keeping quality subscribers on the list, businesses can improve open rates, click-through rates, and ultimately revenue.

Ensuring GDPR Compliance

As mentioned above, businesses that handle personal data from EU residents should ensure that their email marketing practices are GDPR compliant. GDPR mandates that businesses should obtain explicit consent from the users before collecting, processing or using any personal data, including email addresses. Businesses should include an opt-in check box in their sign up forms to obtain consent. Furthermore, updates on policies should be shared with subscribers, and they should be given the option to delete their data altogether.

Avoiding Email Blacklists

Email blacklists are like a "blocklist" of IP addresses and domains that are identified as email spammers. If email marketers are identified as spammers, they may end up on an email blacklist that is used by email clients to filter incoming email messages and label them as spam. If this happens, email deliverability and open rates will be affected, and subscribers will not receive emails. To avoid getting on an email blacklist, businesses should adhere to the anti-spam regulations and best practices for email marketing.

Conclusion

List management and compliance is an essential aspect of email marketing. This chapter highlights the critical elements that businesses should consider when managing email lists, including anti-spam laws, GDPR compliance, and unsubscribe requests. It also discussed the best practices for managing bounces and complaints and avoiding email blacklists. By following these guidelines, businesses can ensure that their email marketing campaigns are targeted, effective, and compliant with the latest regulations.

CHAPTER 7: EMAIL MARKETING INTEGRATION

Email marketing can be an effective way to reach your target audience, but it works best when it's used in conjunction with other marketing channels. Integrating your email marketing with other channels will allow you to reach your audience through multiple touchpoints and create a cohesive brand experience.

In this chapter, we will discuss how to integrate your email marketing with other marketing channels. From social media to SMS and push notifications, we'll explore how to combine email with other channels to create a powerful marketing strategy.

Connecting Email Marketing with Social Media

Social media has become an integral part of any digital marketing strategy, and it can be a great way to complement your email marketing efforts. By connecting your email marketing with social media, you can amplify your message and reach more people.

One effective way to connect email and social media is to include social media buttons in your email templates. This allows subscribers to share your content with their own followers, making it easier to expand your reach.

Another way to integrate email and social media is to promote your email list on social media channels. You can create social media posts encouraging people to sign up for your email list in exchange for a lead magnet, such as an eBook or whitepaper.

Additionally, you can create social media campaigns that align with your email campaigns. For example, if you're promoting a new product in your email campaign, you can create social media ads or posts that highlight the same product.

Integrating with CRM Systems

Customer Relationship Management (CRM) systems are an important tool for managing customer relationships and tracking customer interactions. By integrating your email marketing with your CRM, you can streamline your communication with customers and create a more personalized experience.

One way to integrate email and CRM is to sync your email marketing platform with your CRM system. This allows you to automatically update customer information in your CRM based on their email activity, such as website visits and purchases.

You can also use your CRM data to segment your email list and create targeted email campaigns. By leveraging CRM data such as customer preferences and behavior, you can create emails that are more personalized and relevant to your audience.

Automation tools like Zapier can be used to connect your email marketing platform with your CRM system. This allows you to automate workflows and create triggers based on customer behavior.

Automating SMS and Push Notification Campaigns

SMS and push notifications are another way to communicate with your audience, and integrating them with your email marketing can create a more cohesive marketing strategy. By automating SMS and push notification campaigns based on email activity, you can create a seamless customer experience.

For example, you can create a welcome email series that includes push notifications and SMS messages to encourage engagement. You can also use SMS and push notifications to remind customers of upcoming promotions or deadlines.

Chatbots are another tool that can be used in email marketing integration. For example, you can set up a chatbot that responds to customer inquiries via email, SMS, or push notifications.

Whether you're using SMS, push notifications, or chatbots, it's important to ensure your messages are consistent with your brand voice and messaging. This will create a consistent brand experience across all channels and help build trust with your audience.

Conclusion

Email marketing can be a powerful tool for reaching your audience, but it's most effective when it's used in conjunction with other marketing channels. By integrating email marketing with social media, CRM systems, and other channels, you can create a cohesive marketing strategy that reaches your audience through multiple touchpoints.

Remember, it's important to keep your messaging consistent across all channels to create a seamless customer experience. By doing so, you can build brand loyalty and drive engagement with your audience.

CHAPTER 8: EMAIL MARKETING BEST PRACTICES

Email marketing is one of the most customer-centric marketing channels out there. It allows businesses to reach out to their customers in a direct and personalized manner, offering a great deal of flexibility and customization.

However, it is important to note that users are inundated with an overwhelming amount of emails every day. And if their inboxes are filled with poor or irrelevant content, they are more likely to unsubscribe or mark them as spam.

Therefore, it is essential to follow best practices when it comes to designing and creating email campaigns that can capture and retain the user's attention.

Keep Your Email List Engaged

High-quality, targeted email campaigns that resonate with the user are the key to keeping them engaged with your brand. Sending emails that your subscribers don't want can generate either no response, spam complaints, or unsubscribe requests.

However, following some best practices can help keep subscribers engaged and lessen the likelihood that they'll disengage from your brand.

One of the most effective ways to keep subscribers engaged is by sending regular emails with a compelling content mix that can drive incremental revenue, such as personalized recommendations, highlight upcoming sales, or exclusive offers.

Another way to keep subscribers engaged is by keeping your emails visually appealing using fonts, formatting, and images. Starting your email campaign with an engaging headline can also enhance user engagement.

Personalize Your Emails

Personalization is a powerful tool that can help to create a personalized experience for your subscribers. Personalized emails can deliver content that subscribers are more likely to engage with, increasing open rates, click-through rates, and ultimately conversions.

Some personalization tips that can make your emails more effective are:

➢ Personalizing email subject lines with the subscriber's name

➢ Tailoring email content to the subscriber based on their purchasing history, browsing history, location or behavior

➢ Customizing content based on inferred preferences

Employing Urgency and Scarcity Tactics

Employing urgency and scarcity tactics is a proven way to increase conversions and revenue from email marketing campaigns. A sense of urgency compels customers to take action and make a purchase before the offer or promotion expires.

The use of scarcity tactics, such as exclusive offers to a limited few adds a sense of exclusivity that can motivate customers to subscribe to your mailing list, thus creating more leads.

According to a study by MarketingSherpa, adding time-bound messaging to an email increased click-through rates by 46%.

Using Social Proof in Emails

Social proof is the psychological concept that people tend to believe the behavior and opinions of those around them. The concept of social proof is essential in email marketing campaigns since users prefer to hear from someone they trust.

There are several ways to add social proof to an email, such as adding customer reviews or ratings, user-generated content, and any testimonials. It helps to demonstrate your brand's social reputation and provide the user with a level of comfort in deciding to take the desired action.

Consistency and Frequency

It is important to keep the frequency of sending emails consistent as long gaps between emails can cause subscribers to lose interest.

Consistency in frequency helps build in their minds a specific timeline in which your email is worth opening, thereby increasing engagement. Make sure to provide a variety of content mix in your emails, keeping users uninterested to reduce chances of blocklisting.

Driving Engagement with Interactive Elements

Interactive email elements are a fantastic way to increase engagement with your brand. Interactive elements can transform a static email into a dynamic, engaging experience that captures users' attention.

Adding interactive elements such as videos, quizzes, surveys, and interactive images can increase engagement and ultimately improve campaign ROI.

Building Brand Loyalty

Effective email marketing campaigns can form a direct relationship between you and the subscriber. By offering subscribers a personalized experience, including exclusive deals and personalized content, you can build brand loyalty over time.

Loyal customers tend to engage with your brand more, provide you with free marketing, and also spend more over time on your products or services.

Ensuring Accessibility for All Subscribers

Email marketing campaigns must be accessible to users with different abilities. Accessibility means making your content available to users regardless of any visual, auditory, or physical limitations.

This can include simple practices such as using image alt-tags, avoiding CAPTCHA codes, increasing font size, and avoiding color contrasts that are difficult for certain individuals to read.

Email marketing provides businesses with a unique way of building up their customer base and reaching out to customers effectively. By following the best practices outlined above, businesses can increase the effectiveness of their email marketing campaigns.

This will improve the subscriber experience and ultimately lead to increased engagement, conversion rates, and ROI for the business.

CHAPTER 9: LEAD NURTURING

Lead nurturing is the process of building relationships with potential customers through various channels, such as email, in order to turn them into loyal customers. This process is crucial for businesses looking to increase their conversions and sales. In this chapter, we will discuss the lead nurturing process, creating a lead nurturing strategy, creating effective lead magnets, crafting lead nurturing emails, understanding buyer personas, developing content for each stage of the funnel, and automated lead nurturing.

Understanding the Lead Nurturing Process

The lead nurturing process involves identifying potential customers, providing them with relevant information, and moving them towards making a purchase. It usually consists of three stages: awareness, consideration, and decision-making.

During the awareness stage, you introduce your company to potential customers and provide them with information about your products or services. At this stage, you need to focus on gaining their trust and establishing your brand as an authority in your industry.

In the consideration stage, potential customers start comparing your brand to others and evaluating what you have to offer. They may be interested in your products or services, but they need more information to make an informed decision. This is the stage where you need to provide them with more detailed information about your products, such as case studies and customer reviews.

The decision-making stage is when potential customers are ready to make a purchase. At this stage, you need to provide them with a clear call-to-action and make it easy for them to purchase your products or services.

Creating a Lead Nurturing Strategy

To create an effective lead nurturing strategy, you need to have a clear understanding of your target audience and their buying behavior. You also need to understand their pain points and the challenges they are facing. This will help you tailor your messaging and content to their needs and interests.

When creating a lead nurturing strategy, consider the following:

- ❖ Segment your email list: Divide your email list into different segments based on demographics, interests, and behavior. This will help you send targeted messages to each group and improve your conversion rates.

- ❖ Develop a lead scoring model: A lead scoring model helps you assess the readiness of a lead to make a purchase. It is based on their behavior, such as their engagement with your company or their interactions with your website.

- ❖ Create effective lead magnets: Lead magnets are incentives that you offer to potential customers in exchange for their contact information. They can include whitepapers, eBooks, webinars, and free trials.

- ❖ Craft lead nurturing emails: Lead nurturing emails are designed to move potential customers through the different stages of the marketing funnel. They should be personalized, engaging, and provide value to the recipient.

❖ Develop content for each stage of the marketing funnel: Create content that is relevant to each stage of the marketing funnel. This can include blog posts, case studies, and social media posts.

❖ Implement automated lead nurturing: Use automation tools to send targeted messages to potential customers at the right time. This will help you save time and improve your conversion rates.

Developing Lead Scoring Models

Lead scoring helps you determine which leads are most likely to make a purchase. It involves assigning points to leads based on their behavior, such as opening emails, clicking on links, and visiting your website. A lead scoring model helps you identify the leads that are most likely to convert into paying customers.

When creating a lead scoring model, consider the following:

➢ Define your criteria: Determine the criteria that are most important for scoring leads. This can include their engagement with your company, the actions they take on your website, and their demographic information.

➢ Assign point values: Assign points to each criterion based on its importance. For example, visiting a pricing page may be worth more points than visiting a blog post.

➢ Calculate lead scores: Use a spreadsheet or a marketing automation tool to calculate lead scores based on the criteria and point values you have defined.

➢ Refine your model: Monitor the results of your lead scoring model and refine it as needed. This will help you improve your conversion rates and focus on the leads that are most likely to make a purchase.

Creating Effective Lead Magnets

Lead magnets are incentives that you offer to potential customers in exchange for their contact information. They can be used to build your email list and nurture leads towards making a purchase. When creating lead magnets, consider the following:

> ➤ Provide value: A lead magnet must provide value to the recipient. It should solve a problem or provide a solution to a challenge they are facing.

> ➤ Make it easy to consume: A lead magnet should be easy to consume. It can be a PDF, a video, or an audio file.

> ➤ Use strong headlines: Use strong headlines to grab the recipient's attention and persuade them to download the lead magnet.

> ➤ Promote your lead magnet: Promote your lead magnet on your website, social media, and other channels to attract more leads.

Crafting Lead Nurturing Emails

Lead nurturing emails are designed to move potential customers through the different stages of the marketing funnel. They should be personalized, engaging, and provide value to the recipient. When crafting lead nurturing emails, consider the following:

> ➤ Personalize your emails: Use the recipient's name and other relevant information to personalize your messages. This will help you establish a connection with the recipient and improve your conversion rates.

> ➤ Keep it short and simple: Lead nurturing emails should be short and simple. They should focus on one topic and provide a clear call-to-action.

> ➤ Provide value: Lead nurturing emails should provide value

to the recipient. They can include educational content, case studies, and customer success stories.

➤ Automate your emails: Use automation tools to send targeted messages to potential customers at the right time. This will help you save time and improve your conversion rates.

Understanding Buyer Personas

Understanding your buyer personas is essential for creating effective lead nurturing campaigns. Buyer personas are fictional representations of your ideal customers. They include information such as demographics, interests, and behavior.

When developing your buyer personas, consider the following:

➤ Conduct market research: Conduct market research to understand the needs and interests of your target audience.

➤ Analyze your existing customers: Analyze your existing customers to identify common characteristics and pain points.

➤ Use social media: Use social media to learn more about your target audience's behavior and interests.

➤ Create detailed profiles: Create detailed profiles for each buyer persona, including information such as demographics, job titles, and buying behavior.

Developing Content for Each Stage of the Funnel

Creating content that is relevant to each stage of the marketing funnel is crucial for lead nurturing. Content can include blog posts, case studies, and social media posts. When developing content for each stage of the funnel, consider the following:

➢ Awareness stage: Create content that introduces your company and offers value to your target audience. This can include blog posts, social media posts, and infographics.

➢ Consideration stage: Create content that provides more detailed information about your products or services. This can include case studies, customer reviews, and webinars.

➢ Decision-making stage: Create content that encourages potential customers to make a purchase. This can include testimonials, special offers, and clear calls-to-action.

Automated Lead Nurturing

Automated lead nurturing allows you to send targeted messages to potential customers at the right time. It can include welcome emails, abandoned cart emails, and promotional emails. When implementing automated lead nurturing, consider the following:

➢ Map out your customer journey: Map out your customer journey and identify the different touchpoints where you can use automation.

➢ Use personalization: Use personalization to make your automated messages more relevant and engaging.

➢ Monitor results: Monitor the results of your automated lead nurturing campaigns and refine them as needed.

Conclusion

Lead nurturing is the process of building relationships with potential customers through various channels, such as email, in order to turn them into loyal customers. It involves understanding the marketing funnel, developing effective lead magnets, crafting lead nurturing emails, understanding buyer personas, and developing content for each stage of the funnel. Automated lead nurturing allows you to save time and improve your conversion rates. By implementing an effective lead nurturing strategy, you can increase your sales and grow your business.

CHAPTER 10:
EMAIL CAMPAIGN
OPTIMIZATION

Despite having a well-designed and engaging email marketing campaign, sometimes it may not deliver the expected results. That's why it's essential to develop an optimization strategy to improve your email campaign's overall performance. In this chapter, we will discuss various methods to optimize your email campaigns for better results.

Identifying opportunities for optimization

Optimizing email campaigns isn't possible without identifying areas that require improvement. Sometimes it's the subject line, the layout of the email, the call-to-action, or the timing of the email that requires optimization. An email audit can help identify areas that require improvement.

Analyzing campaign performance

Analyzing campaign performance gives insights into the email campaign's overall performance and the areas that require improvement. Metrics such as open rates, click-through rates, conversion rates, and bounce rates provide data on the overall effectiveness of the email campaign. Analyzing metrics can provide insights into the target audience's preferences, allowing marketers to tailor future campaigns to the target audience.

Conducting an email audit

An email audit is a comprehensive review of the email campaign that examines all elements, including the design, content, and data. This audit identifies areas that require improvement, including the subject line, the design, and the content. An email audit should be carried out regularly to maintain the email campaign's effectiveness.

Enhancing email design

The design of the email plays a critical role in the email campaign's overall success. An email that is visually appealing with images and videos will engage subscribers' attention. An email's design should be optimized for different devices, including mobile devices. Ensuring that the email campaign is mobile-responsive is essential as most subscribers view emails on their mobile devices.

Improving subject lines

The subject line is the first thing the subscriber sees; hence it plays a vital role in determining whether the email will be opened or reduced to the trash folder. A compelling subject line should pique the subscriber's interest and encourage them to open the email. Testing different subject lines is a great way to identify what works best for your subscribers.

Optimizing calls-to-action

An optimized call-to-action should be clear and compelling. The call-to-action should be the email's primary focus, and it should be positioned in a visible place to make it easy for subscribers to act. The placement of the call-to-action should be tested to identify what works best for subscribers.

Testing email timings

Emails sent at the wrong time or day can reduce an email campaign's overall effectiveness. Running tests on email timings can help identify the peak time for subscribers when they are likely to engage with promotional emails.

Enhancing mobile responsiveness

Mobile devices are the primary device for checking emails. Emails designed for desktops only may not display correctly on mobile devices, making them hard to read. Optimizing a campaign for mobile responsiveness is essential to improve the overall effectiveness of the email campaign.

Conclusion

Optimizing an email campaign is an ongoing process for any business looking to improve engagement with its subscribers. Conducting an email audit, analyzing campaign metrics, testing calls-to-action and subject lines, and optimizing mobile responsiveness, and email timings are all strategies that businesses can employ to improve their email campaigns. By continuously monitoring and optimizing email campaigns, businesses can ensure that their email engagements remain engaged and that their email campaigns remain effective.

CHAPTER 11: ADVANCED EMAIL TECHNIQUES

Email marketing can be a highly effective tool for businesses to reach out to their target audience and generate leads. However, with the increasing competition in the market, it is essential to stay ahead of the game and experiment with advanced techniques to make your email campaigns stand out. In this chapter, we will explore some of the advanced email techniques that can help take your email marketing game to the next level.

Utilizing advanced segmentation techniques:

Segmentation is a fundamental aspect of email marketing, and it involves dividing your email list into smaller groups based on various factors such as demographics, behavior, and preferences. While basic segmentation is effective, advanced segmentation techniques take it a step further by creating more personalized and targeted email campaigns. Advanced segmentation involves several factors such as purchasing behavior, customer feedback, and geographic location.

Dynamic content:

Another advanced email marketing technique is incorporating

dynamic content into your email campaigns. Dynamic content refers to individualized content that changes based on the recipient's behavior or preferences. It can include personalized product recommendations, location-specific offers, and dynamic images based on a customer's recent searches.

Personalized image and video:

Images and videos can help make your email campaigns stand out and drive higher engagement rates. However, incorporating personalized images and videos can make it even more effective. For instance, you can use personalized videos that show the customer's name or include images of the recipient's favorite products.

Utilizing AMP for email:

Accelerated Mobile Pages (AMP) are an open-source coding standard that assists in creating fast-loading webpages and email campaigns. AMP for email enables businesses to create interactive and dynamic email campaigns within their inbox, allowing customers to take action without leaving their email client.

Interactive email elements:

Interactive email elements, such as surveys, quizzes, and polls, can help increase customer engagement rates and provide valuable insights about their preferences. These elements encourage customers to take action and provide feedback, leading to better segmentation and personalization.

Developing gamification emails:

Gamification involves incorporating game mechanics into non-game experiences, such as email campaigns, to make them more engaging. Gamification can involve elements such as quizzes, puzzles, and challenges that are tied to rewards or incentives that can help drive customer engagement and loyalty.

Employing machine learning and AI:

Machine learning and Artificial Intelligence (AI) can help businesses automate and improve their email marketing campaigns. For instance, machine learning algorithms can analyze customer behavior, such as purchase history and open rates, to predict future behavior and automate tailored email campaigns.

Setting up triggered emails:

Triggered emails are automated emails that are sent to customers based on specific triggers or actions, such as abandoning their cart or subscribing to a service. These emails can be highly personalized and can encourage customers to take action or make a purchase.

Conclusion:

As email marketing competition continues to increase, it's essential to keep up with the latest trends and experiment with advanced email techniques. Implementing advanced segmentation techniques, dynamic content, personalized images and videos, utilizing AMP, interactive email elements, and gamification can help take your email campaigns to the next level. Employing machine learning and AI and setting up triggered emails can also help drive engagement and conversions. By consistently updating and analyzing your email marketing strategy, businesses can stay ahead of the competition and reap the rewards of successful email marketing campaigns.

CHAPTER 12: EMAIL MARKETING METRICS

In today's world, data is king. And when it comes to email marketing, data takes centre stage. Understanding email marketing metrics is crucial to determining the effectiveness of your email campaigns and making informed decisions moving forward. In this chapter, we'll dive into the different email marketing metrics you need to know to measure your success.

Open Rate Metrics

The open rate metric is one of the most basic and essential email marketing metrics. It's the percentage of people who opened your email out of the total number of emails sent. It's usually calculated by dividing the number of email opens by the number of emails delivered and then multiplying by 100. High open rates indicate that your subject lines are effective and that your audience is interested in your content. However, open rates can be influenced by factors like spam filters, preheader text, and sender reputation. Therefore, it's essential to consider other email marketing metrics when examining the performance of your emails.

Click-Through Rates Metrics

The click-through rate metric measures the percentage of clicks made on the links within your email. It's calculated by dividing the number of clicks by the number of emails delivered and then multiplying by 100. High click-through rates typically indicate that your email content is relevant, engaging, and valuable to your audience. However, low click-through rates can be caused by factors like poorly optimized calls-to-action, a lack of personalization, and irrelevant content. Examining click-through rate metrics can help you pinpoint the areas of improvement in your email campaigns.

Conversion Rates Metrics

Conversion rate metrics measure the percentage of people who took the desired action after clicking through your email. The desired action can be anything from making a purchase to filling out a form to subscribing to your blog. It's calculated by dividing the number of conversions by the number of clicks and then multiplying by 100. A high conversion rate indicates that your email campaign is successful in achieving its goals. However, low conversion rates can be caused by a lack of relevance, unclear calls-to-action, and poor landing page optimization. Examining conversion rate metrics can also help you track the ROI (return on investment) of your email campaigns.

Unsubscribe Rate Metrics

The unsubscribe rate metric measures the number of people who unsubscribed from your email list after receiving an email. It's calculated by dividing the number of unsubscribes by the number of emails delivered and then multiplying by 100. High unsubscribe rates can indicate that your email content is not relevant or valuable to your audience. It's essential to keep your unsubscribe rate as low as possible by maintaining a clean email list and sending relevant content to your subscribers.

Revenue Metrics

Revenue metrics are one of the most critical email marketing metrics for e-commerce businesses. It measures the amount of revenue generated from your email campaigns. It's calculated by multiplying the number of conversions by the average revenue per customer. It helps you determine the impact of your email campaigns on your overall business revenue and can be used to track the ROI of each campaign.

Engagement Metrics

Engagement metrics measure the level of engagement of your audience with your email content. It includes metrics like the time spent reading the email, the number of shares or forwards, and the number of replies. By examining engagement metrics, you can determine the content that resonates most with your audience and adjust your strategy accordingly.

Bounce Rates Metrics

Bounce rate metrics measure the number of emails that were not delivered to the intended recipient. It's calculated by dividing the number of emails that bounced back by the number of emails sent and then multiplying by 100. Bounced emails can be caused by factors like invalid email addresses, full inboxes, and technical issues. It's essential to keep your bounce rate as low as possible by maintaining a clean email list.

Conclusion

Email marketing metrics are essential to measuring the success of your email campaigns. By analyzing open rates, click-through rates, conversion rates, unsubscribe rates, revenue metrics, engagement metrics, and bounce rates, you can determine the effectiveness of your campaigns and make data-driven decisions moving forward. Remember, email marketing is not a set-it-and-forget-it strategy. Continuously monitoring and optimizing your campaigns using email marketing metrics are essential to achieve the best results.

CHAPTER 13:
EMAIL MARKETING AUTOMATION

Email marketing automation is a powerful tool used by businesses of all sizes to grow their customer base, increase revenue, and streamline their marketing efforts. Rather than manually sending out individual emails, automation allows you to set up email campaigns that trigger based on certain conditions or actions taken by the recipient.

Understanding Email Marketing Automation

Email marketing automation can be defined as the use of software to automate certain aspects of an email marketing campaign. This can include triggered emails, lead nurturing workflows, welcome series, abandoned cart emails, and more.

Automation saves businesses time and resources by allowing them to set up email campaigns that are triggered by certain actions taken by the recipient. For example, an abandoned cart email can be sent to a customer who leaves items in their online shopping cart without completing the checkout process. This email can be set up to send automatically within a certain time frame after the customer abandons their cart.

Creating Automation Workflows

Before you can start automating your email campaigns, you need to identify the triggers that will initiate the automated emails. These triggers can be a specific customer action (such as a purchase), a certain date (such as a birthday), or a certain behavior (such as a certain amount of time spent on a website).

Once you have identified the triggers, you can create automation workflows that will send out emails based on these triggers. For example, a triggered email can be set up to send to a customer who hasn't made a purchase in a certain amount of time. The email can offer a discount code to incentivize the customer to make a purchase.

Trigger-based Automation

Trigger-based automation is the most common type of email marketing automation. This type of automation can be used to send out welcome emails to new subscribers, abandoned cart emails to customers who leave items in their cart, and re-engagement emails to subscribers who haven't engaged with your emails in a while.

Trigger-based automation sends out emails based on specific triggers that are set up in advance. For example, an abandoned cart email can be triggered when a customer adds items to their cart but doesn't complete the purchase.

Time-based Automation

Time-based automation sends out emails at regular intervals, such as weekly or monthly updates. This type of automation is often used for newsletter campaigns and can be used to keep subscribers engaged with your content.

Behavioral Automation

Behavioral automation sends out emails based on the behavior of the recipient. For example, a customer who has purchased from your business in the past may receive a follow-up email with product recommendations based on their past purchases.

Creating Drip Campaigns

Drip campaigns are a type of automation that sends out a series of emails over a certain period of time. Drip campaigns can be used for a variety of purposes, such as lead nurturing, onboarding new customers, and offering a special promotion.

Drip campaigns are a great way to keep subscribers engaged with your brand over a longer period of time. The key to creating a successful drip campaign is to provide value with each email, rather than simply trying to sell something in every email.

Lead Nurturing Automation

Lead nurturing is the process of building relationships with potential customers over time. Lead nurturing automation helps to automate this process and deliver targeted, personalized content to each lead based on where they are in the sales funnel.

Lead nurturing automation uses data to provide personalized content to each lead, based on their interests and behavior on your website. This can include personalized recommendations, targeted promotions, and educational content that helps to move the lead through the sales funnel.

Abandoned Cart Automation

Abandoned cart automation is a type of automation that sends out an email to customers who leave items in their shopping cart without completing the purchase. These emails can include a reminder of the items in the cart, an incentive to complete the purchase (such as a discount code), and a call-to-action button to return to the shopping cart.

Abandoned cart automation can have a significant impact on e-commerce sales, as it helps to recover potential lost revenue by reminding customers of items left in their cart.

Conclusion

Email marketing automation is a powerful tool that can help businesses save time and resources, grow their customer base, and increase revenue. By setting up triggered emails, drip campaigns, and other types of automation, businesses can deliver targeted, personalized content to their subscribers and customers.

To get started with email marketing automation, businesses should identify their triggers and create automation workflows that deliver value to their subscribers. By providing targeted content based on the recipient's behavior, businesses can build long-term relationships with their customers, and keep them engaged with their brand over time.

CHAPTER 14: SEGMENTING EMAIL LISTS

Segmentation is one of the most effective ways to increase the engagement and conversion rates of your email marketing campaigns. By segmenting your email list, you can send highly targeted and personalized messages to your subscribers based on their interests, behaviors, location, and demographics. In this chapter, we'll discuss the different types of segmentation, how to segment your email list, and best practices for segmentation.

Understanding Segmentation

Segmentation is the process of dividing your email list into small groups based on certain criteria. These criteria can be demographic, geographic, psychographic, or behavioral. Demographic segmentation includes factors such as age, gender, income, and education. Geographic segmentation includes factors such as location, city, state, or country. Psychographic segmentation includes factors such as values, interests, and lifestyle. Behavioral segmentation includes factors such as purchase history, engagement, and website activity.

Types of Segmentation

There are several types of segmentation that you can use to

segment your email list.

- ➢ Demographic Segmentation - This type of segmentation divides your email list based on demographic data such as age, gender, income, and education.

- ➢ Geographic Segmentation - This type of segmentation divides your email list based on location, city, state, or country.

- ➢ Psychographic Segmentation - This type of segmentation divides your email list based on values, interests, and lifestyle.

- ➢ Behavioral Segmentation - This type of segmentation divides your email list based on purchase history, engagement, and website activity.

- ➢ Custom Segmentation - This type of segmentation creates custom segments based on specific criteria that are unique to your business.

- ➢ Dynamic Segmentation - This type of segmentation divides your email list based on real-time data such as recent website activity, engagement, or purchase history.

Best Practices for Segmentation

- ➢ Define your segmentation criteria - Before you segment your email list, define your segmentation criteria based on your business goals and target audience. Consider factors such as purchase history, website activity, engagement, and demographics.

- ➢ Use a reliable email marketing software - To successfully segment your email list, you need a reliable email marketing platform that allows you to create custom segments and send targeted messages.

➢   Collect relevant data - To segment your email list effectively, you need relevant data on your subscribers. Encourage them to fill out their profile data by offering incentives such as exclusive content or discounts.

➢   Test your segments - Before sending out your email campaign, test your segments to make sure they are accurate and relevant. A/B test your segments to see which ones perform best.

➢ Personalize your messages - Personalization is essential to successful segmentation. Use data from your segments to personalize your email subject lines, content, and calls-to-action.

➢   Monitor and analyze your results - Monitor and analyze your email campaign results to see how your segments performed. Use this data to tweak your segmentation and improve your future campaigns.

Conclusion

Segmentation is a powerful tool that can help you increase your email marketing engagement and conversion rates. By dividing your email list into smaller targeted groups, you can send personalized messages that resonate with your subscribers and encourage them to take action. Use the best practices above to segment your email list effectively and create successful email campaigns.

CHAPTER 15: EMAIL CAMPAIGN PERSONALIZATION

Personalization has become an increasingly important aspect of email marketing. It allows businesses to create a sense of familiarity and connection with their subscribers, resulting in higher engagement rates and ultimately, increased sales. In this chapter, we will discuss the importance of personalization, the data needed for personalization, and tips for personalizing subject lines, email content, images, and videos, and offers and promotions.

The Importance of Personalization

Personalization allows businesses to tailor their messaging to their target audience on a one-to-one basis. It helps to create a connection between the brand and the subscriber, resulting in increased engagement rates and a higher likelihood of conversions. People are more likely to engage with content that is relevant to them, and personalization is the key to achieving this.

Data for Personalization

The first step in personalizing your email campaigns is to collect data about your subscribers. This data can include demographic information such as age, gender, location, and occupation, as well as psychographic information such as interests and hobbies. You can also collect behavioral data such as past purchase history, website activity, and email engagement rates.

The key is to use this data to create segments of subscribers that you can personalize your messaging for. For example, if you have subscribers who have previously purchased from your website, you can create a segment for these subscribers and personalize your messaging accordingly.

Personalizing Subject Lines

The subject line is the first thing that subscribers see when they receive your email. It is crucial to personalize your subject lines to ensure that they stand out in a crowded inbox. Personalization can include using the subscriber's first name or referencing their past purchase history.

For example, using a subject line like "Hey John, we thought you'd love this new product" is more likely to catch John's attention than a generic subject line like "Check out our new product".

Personalizing Email Content

Dynamic content is a great way to personalize your email content. Dynamic content refers to content that changes based on the subscriber's data and behavior. For example, if you have a subscriber who has previously purchased products in a certain category, you can personalize your email content to showcase products in that category.

Additionally, using the subscriber's first name in the email body and addressing them directly can help to create a personalized experience that is more likely to engage the subscriber.

Personalizing Images and Videos

Images and videos are a great way to make an impact with your subscribers, but they are even more effective when they are personalized. You can use subscriber data to dynamically display images and videos that are relevant to the subscriber.

For example, if you are promoting a new line of clothing, you can use subscriber data to display images of clothing items that are relevant to their style or preferences.

Personalizing Offers and Promotions

Offering personalized promotions and discounts can be a great way to drive engagement and sales. For example, you can offer a discount to subscribers who have previously purchased from your site, or offer a free gift to subscribers who reach a certain purchase threshold.

Hyper-personalization takes this a step further by using subscriber data to offer promotions and discounts that are unique to each subscriber. For example, if you have a subscriber who has shown an interest in a particular product, you can offer them a discount on that product.

Employing Dynamic Personalization

Dynamic personalization refers to the use of subscriber data to personalize content and offers in real-time. This can include dynamically displaying products that are relevant to the subscriber or customizing offers and promotions based on the subscriber's behavior and data.

For example, you can use dynamic personalization to display real-time inventory levels for products that the subscriber has shown interest in, or offer a discount on a product that the subscriber has viewed but not purchased.

Implementing Hyper-personalization

Hyper-personalization takes personalization to an entirely new level. It uses advanced data analysis and machine learning algorithms to offer recommendations and promotions that are unique to each subscriber.

For example, Amazon utilizes hyper-personalization in their email marketing by offering product recommendations based on a subscriber's past purchase history and browsing behavior. They also use personalized messaging to encourage subscribers to complete their purchase by displaying the products in their cart, as well as related products that the subscriber may be interested in.

Conclusion

Personalization is no longer an option for businesses, it's a necessity. By using subscriber data to create personalized messaging, businesses can tailor their content to their target audience on a one-to-one basis, resulting in increased engagement rates, higher sales, and greater customer loyalty.

Employing dynamic personalization and hyper-personalization can take personalization to an entirely new level, creating a truly unique and personalized experience for each subscriber. By leveraging these advanced personalization techniques, businesses can stand out in a crowded inbox and build meaningful connections with their subscribers.

CHAPTER 16: ADVANCED EMAIL MARKETING STRATEGIES

As email marketing continues to evolve, businesses are always looking for new and innovative ways to maximize their reach and engagement with their customers. In this chapter, we will explore some advanced email marketing strategies that businesses can implement to take their campaigns to the next level.

1. Implementing Account-Based Marketing

Account-Based Marketing (ABM) is a strategy that is gaining popularity among B2B marketers. As the name suggests, this approach is all about targeting specific accounts or companies rather than individual customers. The idea is to create highly personalized and targeted campaigns that speak directly to the specific needs and pain points of those businesses.

To implement ABM, businesses must first identify the customer accounts they want to target. They then need to create detailed buyer personas and tailor their email campaigns to those personas. This can include personalized messaging, targeted offers, and relevant content that addresses the specific pain points and challenges of the target accounts.

2. Creating Email Funnels

Email funnels are a series of automated emails that are sent to subscribers based on specific triggers or actions. The purpose of these funnels is to guide the subscriber through the customer journey, from awareness to conversion and beyond.

One example of an email funnel is the welcome series. This is a sequence of emails that are automatically triggered when a subscriber signs up for your list. These emails should introduce the subscriber to your brand, set expectations, and provide valuable content that encourages them to engage with your brand.

Other examples of email funnels include abandoned cart emails, re-engagement campaigns, and post-purchase follow-ups. By creating and optimizing these automated funnels, businesses can engage with customers in a more personalized and effective way.

3. Predictive Email Analytics

Predictive analytics involves using data from past campaigns to predict future results. Predictive email analytics takes this strategy one step further by using customer data and behavior to predict which subscribers are most likely to engage with future campaigns.

To implement predictive email analytics, businesses need to identify the customer behaviors that are most closely associated with engagement. This could include factors like previous engagement with emails, website behavior, and purchase history.

By using this data to predict which subscribers are most likely to engage with future campaigns, businesses can target their email efforts more effectively and maximize their success rates.

4. Email Remarketing

Email remarketing is a strategy that involves targeting subscribers who have shown interest in your brand or products but have not yet converted. This could include subscribers who have abandoned their cart or visited your website but didn't make a purchase.

The goal of email remarketing is to re-engage these subscribers and encourage them to take action. This can be done through targeted email campaigns that offer incentives, address pain points, and provide compelling reasons to convert.

5. Social Media Retargeting via Email

Social media retargeting involves targeting users on social media platforms based on their previous interactions with your brand. This approach can also be used in email marketing by targeting subscribers who have engaged with your brand on social media but have not yet converted.

By incorporating social media retargeting into email campaigns, businesses can increase their reach and engagement with subscribers who are already interested in their brand. This can be done through email campaigns that include social media calls-to-action or by creating targeted social media ads that are designed to complement the email campaigns.

6. Email Partnerships and Sponsorships

Partnering with other businesses and brands can be an effective way to expand your reach and gain new subscribers. By teaming up with complementary brands that share your values and target audience, you can access a wider pool of potential customers.

One way to implement this strategy is through email sponsorships. This involves partnering with another brand to create a joint email campaign that promotes both brands. This can be a win-win scenario for both businesses if the partnership is executed correctly.

7. SMS Marketing Integration

SMS marketing is a powerful channel that can be used in conjunction with email to increase engagement and conversions. By integrating SMS campaigns with email campaigns, businesses can create a multi-channel approach that reaches customers on their preferred channels.

SMS marketing is particularly effective for time-sensitive promotions and urgent notifications. Integrating SMS with email can create a sense of urgency and increase the chances of customers taking action.

8. Email Marketing for B2B

While the principles of email marketing apply to all businesses, B2B marketers face some unique challenges and opportunities. B2B email campaigns need to be highly targeted, personalized, and optimized for specific funnel stages.

B2B email campaigns should focus on lead nurturing, relationship building, and delivering valuable content that addresses the specific pain points and challenges of the business. By taking a strategic and data-driven approach to email marketing, B2B businesses can drive conversions and build long-term relationships with their customers.

In conclusion, advanced email marketing strategies are all about taking a data-driven and innovative approach to campaigns. By implementing these tactics, businesses can expand their reach, increase engagement, and drive conversions in a more personalized and effective way.

CHAPTER 17: EMAIL MARKETING FOR E-COMMERCE

Email marketing is an essential component for e-commerce businesses to connect with their customers. Creating personalized and targeted emails can help improve customer engagement, drive sales, and increase customer loyalty. In this chapter, we will discuss the different types of e-commerce emails, how to create effective campaigns, and the best practices for e-commerce businesses.

Understanding E-commerce Email Marketing

E-commerce email marketing involves creating and sending emails to customers or prospective customers to drive sales, build brand awareness, and increase customer loyalty. E-commerce businesses can use different types of emails to stay in touch with their customers and promote their products or services. These emails include abandoned cart emails, welcome series, product recommendation emails, loyalty program emails, cross-selling emails, upselling emails, and post-purchase emails.

Creating Abandoned Cart Emails

Abandoned cart emails are one of the most important emails for e-commerce businesses. They are sent to customers who have added products to their cart but left the website without making a purchase. Abandoned cart emails aim to remind the customer of the products they have left behind and encourage them to complete their purchase.

Creating compelling subject lines that include the product name, offer, or urgency can help increase open rates. The email should display the products left behind, along with their price, images, and a call-to-action button to encourage customers to complete their purchase. Including customer reviews and testimonials can also help increase conversions.

Welcome Series for E-commerce

The welcome series is a sequence of emails sent to new subscribers who have signed up for an e-commerce store's emails. The series aims to introduce the brand, build trust, and encourage the customer to make a purchase.

The first email in the series can be a welcome email that thanks the customer for signing up and includes a brief introduction to the business. The second email can showcase the store's best-selling products or categories, along with a discount code to encourage the customer to make their first purchase. The third email can be a follow-up email that checks in with the customer and offers additional product recommendations.

Product Recommendation Emails

Product recommendation emails are sent to customers based on their buying behavior and preferences. They suggest products that the customer is likely to be interested in based on their previous purchases or browsing behavior on the website.

To create effective product recommendation emails, businesses can utilize customers' purchase history to create personalized recommendations. The email should include compelling images of the recommended products, their name, price, and a call-to-action button to drive traffic to the website.

Creating Loyalty Programs via Email

E-commerce businesses can use email marketing to create loyalty programs that reward customers for their purchases and encourage them to keep coming back. Loyalty programs can be designed in different ways, such as points systems or exclusive offers, and can be linked to customers' email addresses for easy tracking.

Loyalty program emails should include the customer's current points balance, the rewards they can redeem, and a clear call-to-action to encourage them to make a purchase. It's also important to make the customer feel valued and recognized for their loyalty.

Cross-selling and Upselling via Email

Cross-selling and upselling emails are designed to encourage customers to buy related or higher-priced products they may not have considered before. Cross-selling emails recommend products that complement the customer's previous purchase, while upselling emails recommend higher-priced or more premium options.

To create cross-selling and upselling emails, businesses can use customers' purchase history to recommend related products or suggest products based on their browsing behavior. The email should include compelling images of the recommended products, their name, price, and a call-to-action button to drive traffic to the website.

Creating Post-Purchase Emails

Post-purchase emails are sent to customers after they have made a purchase to thank them for their business, request their feedback, and encourage repeat purchases.

The email should contain a thank-you message, a summary of the customer's purchase, and a call-to-action to encourage them to make a repeat purchase or leave a review. Including a discount or exclusive offer can also help increase customer loyalty.

Utilizing Reviews in Email Marketing

Customer reviews and testimonials can help build trust and social proof for e-commerce businesses. Including reviews in email marketing can help increase conversions and encourage repeat purchases.

Businesses can include customer reviews in their product recommendation emails or post-purchase emails to encourage customers to leave their own review. They can also use reviews in their loyalty program emails to encourage customers to earn rewards by leaving reviews.

Conclusion

Email marketing is an essential tool for e-commerce businesses to connect with their customers and drive sales. Abandoned cart emails, welcome series, product recommendation emails, loyalty program emails, cross-selling emails, upselling emails, and post-purchase emails are all effective types of emails that e-commerce businesses can use. Creating personalized and targeted emails that focus on the customer's needs can help build brand loyalty and increase customer retention.

CHAPTER 18: EMAIL MARKETING FOR B2B

Business-to-business (B2B) marketing differs significantly from business-to-consumer (B2C) marketing. While B2C marketing targets individuals, B2B marketing focuses on other businesses. The primary goal of B2B marketing is to generate leads, nurture them, and convert them into customers. B2B is a complex space, and email marketing plays a vital role in the process. In this chapter, we will discuss some important aspects of B2B email marketing.

Creating Lead Nurturing Workflows

With B2B email marketing, the ultimate goal is to generate leads and convert them into customers. However, reaching that ultimate goal requires a series of steps. Creating a lead nurturing workflow is an essential part of B2B email marketing. The workflow is a series of automated emails that are designed to move prospects through the sales funnel. The workflow is triggered based on the prospect's behavior or actions.

Here is an example of a lead nurturing workflow:

❖ Welcome email: The first email in the workflow is a welcome email. This email sets the tone for the rest of the workflow and introduces the prospect to your company and the products or services you offer.

❖ Educational email: The second email in the workflow is an educational email. This email should provide valuable information to the prospect related to their pain points and offer a solution.

❖ Case study email: The third email in the workflow features a case study. This email should showcase the success of a previous client or customer and how your product or service has helped them.

❖ Product demonstration email: The fourth email in the workflow is a product demonstration email. This email should provide a deeper dive into your product or service and how it could help the prospect's business. You could also offer a free trial or demo.

❖ Final email: The last email in the workflow should be a final offer. It could be a discount or limited-time offer to encourage the prospect to make a purchase.

Creating Event Invitation Emails

Email is one of the most effective ways to invite people to events, whether they are webinars, trade shows, or conferences. Email invitations should be designed to generate interest and excitement, and the messaging should clearly convey the benefits of attending the event. When developing your email invitations, consider the following:

❖ Subject line: Your subject line is the first thing the recipient will see, so it should be compelling enough to encourage them to open the email. Use a benefit-focused subject line to capture their attention.

❖ Messaging: Your email messaging should be persuasive, highlighting the benefits of attending the event. Use persuasive language to create a sense of urgency for the recipient to register.

❖　　Event details: Make sure you provide clear and concise information about the event, including the agenda, the venue, and the date and time.

❖　　Social Proof: Utilize social proof by mentioning the speakers, presenters, or any notable attendees.

❖　　Call-to-action: To encourage the recipient to register, include a clear and concise call-to-action (CTA) that directs them to the registration page.

Using Case Studies and Success Stories

Case studies and success stories are an excellent way to build trust with potential customers. Case studies showcase real-world scenarios where your product or service has helped a business achieve its objectives. They deliver strong evidence that your product or service is effective in solving the problems they are facing. Here are a few tips for creating effective case studies and success stories:

❖　　Interview your clients: Reach out to your clients and ask if they would like to be featured in a case study or success story. Ask them about their experience with your product or service, and how it has helped them achieve their business objectives.

❖　　Highlight the problem: Make sure you clearly identify the problem that your client was facing before they implemented your product or service.

❖　　Showcase the solution: Illustrate how your product or service helped your client solve the problem and achieved their objectives.

❖　　Use quantitative data: Use metrics and data to demonstrate the impact your product or service had on their business.

Creating Whitepapers and eBooks

Whitepapers and eBooks are great lead generation tools for B2B companies. They provide valuable information to potential customers and showcase the company's expertise in the industry they serve. Whitepapers and eBooks are designed to educate the reader and provide in-depth analysis on a particular topic relevant to the industry.

Here are some tips for creating effective whitepapers and eBooks:

- ❖ Identify a topic: Choose a topic that is relevant to your industry and your target audience.

- ❖ Research and analyze: Do extensive research on the topic and provide critical analysis to provide unique insights.

- ❖ Use data and statistics: Use relevant data and statistics to support your argument and provide credibility.

- ❖ Use visuals: Including relevant visuals such as images, infographics, and charts make the whitepaper or eBook more engaging and appealing.

- ❖ Talk to your audience: Use a conversational tone and address your audience directly to make them feel like you are providing value directly to them.

Creating Referral Programs via Email

Referrals are an excellent way to grow your B2B business. Referral programs via email can generate a substantial number of leads for your company. These programs reward existing customers for referring their friends, colleagues, or industry peers.

Here are some tips for creating an effective referral program via email:

➤ Rewards: Offer rewards that will encourage customers to refer your product or service. This could be discount codes, free trials, or even a monetary reward.

➤ Clear instructions: Make sure you provide clear instructions on how to participate in the referral program. Give them a specific link to share with their network to track referrals.

➤ Follow-ups: Follow up with customers who have participated in the referral program to thank them and keep them engaged.

Conclusion

B2B email marketing requires a different approach from B2C email marketing. The goal is to generate leads, nurture them, and convert them into customers. To achieve this goal, B2B marketers need to create effective lead nurturing workflows, event invitation emails, case studies, whitepapers and eBooks, and referral programs via email. With the right strategies in place, B2B email marketing can lead to significant business growth.

CHAPTER 19: EMAIL MARKETING FOR SMALL BUSINESS

Small businesses need effective marketing strategies that can deliver results with a small budget. Email marketing can be a great option for small businesses to communicate with their customers and boost their revenue. In this chapter, we'll explore the best practices and strategies for email marketing for small businesses.

Creating a Small Business Email Marketing Strategy

To create a successful email marketing campaign for your small business, you need to have a good email marketing strategy in place. Here are some essential steps to take:

➢ Define your email marketing goals: Before you start any email campaign, you need to have clear goals in mind. What do you want to achieve with your campaign? Do you want to increase sales, promote your brand, or engage with your customers?

➢ Define your target audience: To make your emails effective, you need to know your target audience. Who are your customers? What are their needs and interests? How can your products or services help them?

➢ Choose an email marketing platform: There are many email marketing platforms available in the market. Choose the one that suits your needs and budget.

➢ Create a content strategy: Plan your email content in advance. What kind of content do you want to send to your subscribers? How often do you want to send emails?

Utilizing Email for Customer Retention

Acquiring new customers is important for the growth of small businesses, but it's equally important to retain your existing customers. Email marketing can be a great tool for customer retention. Here are some best practices to keep in mind:

❖ Welcome emails: When someone signs up for your email list, send them a welcome email that thanks them for joining and introduces your business. This can set the tone for a great customer experience.

❖ Exclusive offers: Offer exclusive discounts or promotions to your email subscribers. This can encourage them to stay subscribed and make future purchases.

❖ Newsletters: Send newsletters to your subscribers with updates about your business, new products, or any other relevant information. This can help to keep your brand top of mind.

❖ Personalization: Personalize your emails to make your subscribers feel valued. Use their name, location, or purchase history to create more personalized messages.

Building Brand Awareness via Email

Email marketing can also be a great tool for building brand awareness. Here are some tips to keep in mind:

❖ Consistency: Be consistent with your email frequency and messaging to create a sense of familiarity with your brand.

❖ Visuals: Use compelling visuals in your emails to capture the attention of your subscribers. Make sure your emails are mobile-friendly with easy-to-read fonts and short paragraphs.

❖ Branding: Be sure to include your company logo and brand colors in your emails. This can help to reinforce your brand identity.

❖ CTAs: Include clear calls-to-action (CTAs) in your emails. This can encourage your subscribers to take action, whether it's making a purchase or visiting your website.

Creating Email-Based Referral Programs

Referral programs can be an excellent way for small businesses to acquire new customers. Here's how to create an effective email-based referral program:

➢ Offer incentives: Offer incentives to your existing customers to refer their friends and family to your business. This can include exclusive discounts, free products, or other rewards.

➢ Make it easy: Make it as easy as possible for your customers to refer others. Include a referral link or code in your emails, and provide clear instructions on how to use it.

➢ Follow up: Once someone is referred to your business, follow up with them via email to thank them for their interest. This can help to create a positive first impression.

Creating Email Newsletters

Email newsletters can be an effective way for small businesses to keep their customers informed and engaged. Here are some tips for creating a great email newsletter:

❖ Keep it short and sweet: Keep your newsletter concise and

to the point. Include only the most important information, and use visuals to make it more engaging.

❖ Provide value: Provide valuable content in your newsletters that your subscribers will be interested in reading. This can include tips, advice, or insights into your business or industry.

❖ Timing: Choose a consistent schedule for your newsletter, whether it's weekly, monthly, or quarterly. Make sure you send your newsletters at a time that's convenient for your subscribers.

❖ Consistency: Be consistent with your branding and messaging in your newsletters. This can help to reinforce your brand identity.

Using Email for Event Promotion

Small businesses can also use email marketing to promote events, whether it's an in-store sale or a community event. Here are some tips to keep in mind:

➢ Early promotion: Start promoting your event via email early, so your subscribers have plenty of time to plan to attend.

➢ Clear messaging: Make sure your email messaging is clear and concise. Highlight the most important details about your event, such as the date, time, and location.

➢ Visuals: Use visual elements in your emails, such as photos or graphics, to make your messages more engaging and memorable.

➢ Follow up: Follow up with your subscribers after the event via email to thank them for attending. This can help to build customer loyalty and encourage repeat business.

Offering Promotions via Email

Finally, small businesses can use email marketing to offer promotions and discounts to their subscribers. Here are some best practices to keep in mind:

❖ Clear messaging: Make sure your promotion messaging is clear, concise, and easy to understand. Highlight the offer in the subject line and keep the email body focused on the promotion.

❖ Limited time: Offer promotions for a limited time, which can encourage your subscribers to act quickly.

❖ Exclusivity: Make your promotions exclusive to email subscribers only. This can incentivize people to sign up for your email list.

❖ High-value offers: Offer promotions that provide real value to your subscribers, such as free shipping or a significant discount. This can help to build customer loyalty and encourage repeat business.

Conclusion

Email marketing can be a powerful tool for small businesses to connect with their customers, build brand awareness, and increase revenue. By implementing the best practices and strategies outlined in this chapter, small businesses can create effective email marketing campaigns that deliver results while working within their budget.

CHAPTER 20: EMAIL MARKETING FOR NON-PROFIT

Email marketing is an essential tool for non-profit organizations that want to engage with donors, volunteers, and supporters. Through email, non-profit organizations can create targeted campaigns that inspire action and build meaningful relationships with their audience.

Understanding Email Marketing for Non-Profit

Email marketing for non-profit organizations is not just about creating a sales pitch or promoting the organization's cause. Instead, it's about building a sense of community and creating a connection that inspires supporters to take action.

Non-profit organizations need to create email campaigns that are emotionally compelling and speak directly to their audience's interests and values. These campaigns should be focused on building relationships, not just soliciting donations.

Creating Email Campaigns for Fundraising

Email is an excellent tool for fundraising. Still, non-profit organizations must approach fundraising campaigns strategically. They must consider the message they want to convey, the audience they want to reach, and the timing of their campaign.

To create an effective fundraising campaign, non-profit organizations must:

1. Clearly Communicate Their Organization's Mission and Goals

Donors want to support non-profit organizations that have a clear mission and goals. Non-profit organizations must articulate their mission and goals in a concise, compelling way that inspires donors to take action.

2. Build a Sense of Urgency

Creating a sense of urgency is vital in fundraising. Non-profit organizations must give prospective donors a reason to donate immediately. This can be achieved by setting a fundraising goal and setting a deadline for donations.

3. Tell a Compelling Story

Telling a compelling story is critical in fundraising. Non-profit organizations must share stories that illustrate the impact of their work and how donations can make a difference.

Creating targeted campaigns for specific donor segments

Non-profit organizations must create targeted campaigns that speak to the interests and values of specific donor segments. This can be achieved by segmenting the email list based on:

1. Giving history

Segmenting donors based on their giving history can help non-profit organizations understand their donors' donation patterns. This information can be used to create campaigns that target specific donation levels or encourage donors to increase their donation amount.

2. Demographics

Demographic information such as age, gender, and location can provide insights into donors' interests and values. This information can be used to create campaigns that speak directly to a specific segment of donors.

3. Interests

Non-profit organizations can use email surveys to learn more about their donors' interests. This information can be used to create campaigns that speak directly to donors' interests and values, increasing the chances of engagement and action.

Utilizing social proof in non-profit emails

Non-profit organizations can use social proof to build trust and credibility with their donors. Social proof can take many forms, including testimonials, success stories, and images or video showing the impact of the organization's work.

Non-profit organizations can also leverage social media to amplify social proof. Sharing success stories, testimonials, and images on social media can help build support, attract new donors, and increase engagement.

Creating volunteer recruitment emails

Volunteers are essential to non-profit organizations. Without volunteers, many non-profit organizations couldn't achieve their mission. Creating volunteer recruitment emails is an effective way for non-profit organizations to solicit support from their audience.

Volunteer recruitment emails should be compelling and include:

- ❖ A clear description of the volunteer opportunity
- ❖ The benefits of volunteering
- ❖ A call-to-action that encourages individuals to sign up to volunteer.

Utilizing email surveys for donor feedback

Email surveys are an effective tool for collecting feedback from donors. Non-profit organizations can use email surveys to gather information on donor interests, the effectiveness of their communication efforts, and satisfaction levels.

Email surveys should be short and focused on specific topics. They should include closed-ended questions, such as multiple-choice questions, to make it easier for donors to respond. Non-profit organizations can also use open-ended questions to gather more in-depth feedback.

Creating email campaigns for spreading awareness

Email can be used as a tool to spread awareness about non-profit organizations and their mission. Non-profit organizations can use email to share stories and information about their work, educate their audience on critical issues, and encourage engagement with their organization.

Creating email campaigns for spreading awareness should be focused on providing value to the recipient. Non-profit organizations should consider including:

- ❖ Educational resources, such as infographics or reports.
- ❖ Inspiring stories that illustrate the impact of their work.

❖ Opportunities for engagement, such as signing petitions or sharing content on social media.

Conclusion

Email marketing is a powerful tool for non-profit organizations that want to build relationships with donors, volunteers, and supporters. By creating emotionally compelling campaigns for fundraising, utilizing social proof, and creating targeted campaigns, non-profit organizations can build meaningful relationships with their audience and achieve their mission. Email marketing can help non-profit organizations reach new audiences, build awareness, and raise funds, allowing them to make a more significant impact in their communities and the world. Email marketing can help your business grow and thrive. With the tips and strategies outlined in this book, you now have the knowledge to create effective email campaigns that engage your audience and drive conversions. Remember to always put yourself in the shoes of your subscribers - what do they want to see from you? What value can you provide them?

It's important to continuously test and analyze your email marketing efforts to see what works best for your specific audience. Don't be afraid to experiment with different subject lines, content formats, and sending times. And most importantly, always prioritize building a strong relationship with your subscribers by providing valuable content and personalized experiences.

As the world of online marketing continues to evolve, email marketing remains a tried-and-true method that delivers results. By using the secrets shared in this book, you can take advantage of this powerful tool and achieve success in growing your business through effective email campaigns.

Thank you for reading Email Marketing Secrets - I hope you found it helpful on your journey towards creating impactful email

RAY GOODWIN

campaigns!

ABOUT THE AUTHOR

Ray Goodwin

Ray Goodwin, is the author behind this series of captivating books on Business Development and self improvement, and has left an indelible mark on the field. He was born and raised in the bustling city of London, where he developed a strong work ethic and an insatiable curiosity about the inner workings of successful businesses. Throughout his illustrious career, Ray leveraged his extensive knowledge and experience to help numerous companies flourish and prosper.

His keen insights and innovative strategies has earned him recognition, driving him to share his expertise with others. Ray believes in the power of sharing knowledge to elevate businesses and empower aspiring entrepreneurs.

Ray's dedication to his craft is evident in the numerous books he has authored on business development and self improvement. His writing style seamlessly blends practical advice, thought-provoking concepts, and real-life case studies, making his books invaluable resources for business professionals and novices alike. His ability to distill complex concepts into accessible language has greatly impacted the lives and careers of countless individuals.

Now retired from the corporate world, Ray and his beloved wife have settled in the idyllic English countryside. Surrounded by the beauty of nature, Ray finds inspiration for his writing and indulges in his hobbies.

Ray Goodwin's books continue to serve as enduring guides for those seeking success in the business world. With a wealth of experience and a deep understanding of the inner workings of businesses, Ray's work remains a testament to his passion for sharing knowledge and helping others flourish.